Some Greek Poems of
Love & Beauty

SOME GREEK POEMS OF
LOVE AND BEAUTY

being a selection from
the Little Things of Greek Poetry
made & translated into English
by

J. M. EDMONDS
Lecturer in the University

CAMBRIDGE
AT THE UNIVERSITY PRESS
1937

CAMBRIDGE
UNIVERSITY PRESS

University Printing House, Cambridge CB2 8BS, United Kingdom

Cambridge University Press is part of the University of Cambridge.

It furthers the University's mission by disseminating knowledge in the pursuit of education, learning and research at the highest international levels of excellence.

www.cambridge.org
Information on this title: www.cambridge.org/9781107554290

© Cambridge University Press 1937

First published 1937
First paperback edition 2015

A catalogue record for this publication is available from the British Library

ISBN 978-1-107-55429-0 Paperback

Contents

Preface

English verse-translations of many of these poems have been made before. While I was making mine, I refrained from looking at others; but this will not have prevented the seeming plagiarisms of subconscious reminiscence and fortuitous similarity. If I am accused of phrase-lifting, I plead either that I didn't mean to or that I couldn't help it. We all aim at the semblance of inevitability, and sometimes what seems inevitable, is. To the reader who asks why I have left out this and that, I would say, first that the choice was mine not his, secondly that it seemed folly to attempt to translate where another's version was part of English literature, and thirdly that there are some delightful little Greek poems which will not go into verse, and yet are too slight to bear rendering into prose.

A few of these translations have been printed before, that of Theocritus' *Distaff* in the *Cambridge Review*, one or two in the *Lyra Graeca* of the Loeb Classical Library (Heinemann), and those of the Sappho fragments in *Sappho Revocata* (Peter Davies). Excepting these and a few which were written in 1929, all are the work of the summer of 1935. Much of my present Introduction has been adapted from that of a selection which was published as *Some Greek Love-Poems* by Mr Peter Davies some years ago.

Among the many kind friends on whom I have tried these verses before having them printed I must thank here Robert Gittings, Arthur Quiller-Couch, Harris Rackham, Nelly Smith-Dampier, Eustace Tillyard, James Vince, and the reader of the University Press. They all will forgive me, I know, for not always taking their advice.

J. M. E.

May 1937

When I lived I sought no wings,
  Schemed no heaven, planned no hell,
But, content with little things,
  Made an earth, and it was well.
Richard Middleton, Pagan Epitaph

The Poets and their Work

In the Greece of the seventh century before Christ the human spirit was fast growing to man's estate. Kings had mostly gone, aristocracies were going, wealth and power, even supreme power, were for any man to win. The patronage of art was passing from the court to the counting-house by way of the town-hall. Homer had told long before of the Heroes, Hesiod more recently of husbandry, both in epic verse which had now begun to lose its once invariable musical accompaniment. Archilochus, Mimnermus, Alcman, in tunes and measures new to the world of art, were now singing to flute or lyre of their own feelings; and the age-long rite of tribal song-dance not only had become a thing of state-encouraged competition, but was adding secular and personal elements to its hieratic theme. Alcman makes his chorus of Spartan girls, with the simple sympathetic vividness of a vase-painting, describe themselves; and describes their trainer in two lines of a *solo* Love-Song which bear the hall-mark of whole-world kinship: 'It is not Aphrodite; but wild Love, like a child, plays me touch-me-not-with-your-little-reed, treading softly on tiptoe.' Here is self-consciousness, individualism, the personal lyric. The world has indeed grown up.

The first portrait-statue—that of a victorious Spartan athlete—appears in 628, the first *Encomium* or Eulogy among the fragments of the Lesbian Alcaeus a few years later. This, the Song-in-the-Revel, came of an old feast-custom akin on the one side to the 'renowns of men' of which Homer tells and whence the Epic grew, and on the other to the traditional Libation-Songs sung to Zeus and the Heroes, and the Paean sung to Apollo. Difference of occasion, at first slight, abetted for us by Alexandrian pedantry, has divided this class of songs, or as they still sometimes were, song-dances, into the Victory-Song, the Drinking-Song, and the Love-Song. The pedigree of the Love-Song is marked by the fragment in which Alcaeus begs his beloved to 'receive your revel-singer', i.e. serenader. The Victory-Song, or song of congratulation to the winner in the Games—how Greek that these should be some of their finest poetry!—is outside our present scope. Translations of most of the extant Drinking-Songs are reserved for a future volume, but not a few will be found in this; for a Greek Drinking-Song did not necessarily concern itself with drinking. In Greek education the learning of poetry by heart took the place which language-study does in ours; and the Greeks did not put away such things as childish when they left school, but sang or recited poems they had learnt there or picked up in later life, whenever their turn came to entertain their fellow-guests. Thus almost any theme was suitable—wealth and poverty, youth and age, virtue and vice, war, friendship, love, marriage, behaviour at table, politics, travel, satire, death.

Archilochus, it is said, 'invented the custom of reciting some of the Iambics to music and singing others'. Here begins, in another sphere than the Epic, the divorce of poetry from song. Before the turn of the century we find at least one of the two Lesbians using the Love-Poem as the love-message. But most of the exquisite (though too often fragmentary) poetry of the great Mytilenean monodists Sappho and Alcaeus, who through their imitators have done more for the poetry of Europe than any man but Homer, was doubtless sung to the music of the lyre; for they employed mainly what in their day and long after were the

[2]

metres *par excellence* of song, the 'tune-metres' as they were called, Melic. For the poetry of love and wine this tradition held, side by side with that of the Elegiac, sung to the flute, and that of the Iambic and Trochaic, whose accompaniment was a kind of lyre, through the century which began with Solon, continued with Stesichorus and Ibycus, and ended with Anacreon. From the Persian Wars near the beginning of the fifth century to the revival of the Lyric Tale by Timotheus towards the end of it, the Melic metre—except for the Dithyramb or song-dance to Dionysus and (later) other Gods—is almost entirely confined to the Choric songs, as the Iambic to the spoken parts, of the Drama; the Elegiac, growing more and more a matter of mere recitation, holds almost undisputed sway over poetry of love and wine until the Alexandrian Age revives the Hexameter and the Anacreontic.

Solon is an example—not unparalleled in early Greece—of the poet who receives full powers to heal public ills. Even his political poems are always poetry. It is clear that he was a statesman because he was a poet, and not *vice versa*. Of another poet-statesman, canonised like him as one of the Seven Sages, Cleobûlus of Lindus in Rhodes, we know that he wrote songs and riddles. The riddle, which, like the pun, enjoyed greater dignity then than it does now, was often an alternative to a song or recitation at table. To the same age belong Demodocus of Leros and Phocylides of Milêtus, writers of satire in epic or elegiac verse. Phocylides' couplet on the little city set upon a high place is alone enough to justify his ancient reputation. Demodocus' lines on Procles imitated by Porson in the famous epigram on Hermann, and his dictum that the Milesians may not be dolts but they behave like dolts, make us wish we had more of him. Of Stesichorus' Doric Love-Songs, though we know he wrote

[3]   A 2

them, we have nothing but a few names and plots which indicate that they were impersonal, Lyric Tales taken, it would seem, from the lips of the people and sung to the lyre by a single performer to the accompaniment of a dancing chorus. His later contemporary Ibycus, who refused the offered 'tyranny' of his native city, the half-Doric half-Ionic Rhegium, and withdrew to Samos, there to live under Aiaces and his son Polycrates, is the first court-poet we hear of after the Heroic Age. If we had more of his work, this once famous man would perhaps rank as the 'male Sappho'. Like Sappho's, some at least of his poems were Choric. At the same court, and later at the court of the Pisistratids at Athens, lived the great Ionian monodic singer of love and wine—and old age—Anacreon, whose modern fame rests, for all but those who know the fine few remnants of his own work, on poems inspired by his in late Alexandrian and Roman times. It speaks much both for Anacreon and for his public that Pausanias could write in the second century of our era: 'On the Athenian Acropolis there are statues of Pericles son of Xanthippus and of his father also who fought the Persians at Mycalè: near Xanthippus stands Anacreon of Teos, the first poet excepting Sappho of Lesbos to make his chief theme love; the statue represents him as one singing in his cups.' Alcaeus has been called the Greek Byron; Anacreon may more justly, though with many reservations, be called the Greek Burns.

In the Song-Book, or rather Song-Books, which have come down to us under the name of Theognis of Megara, we have probably the remains of a late sixth-century collection, added to in the fifth, of his own and some others' convivial poetry—taking this term to include all poetry suitable for singing or reciting at table. It is written entirely

[4]

in the Elegiac metre. Among much that is unattractive to us, though never second-rate, there are some fine Love-Poems. A Song-Book of slightly later date is the collection known as *Athenian Drinking-Songs* preserved in whole or part by Athenaeus. This, which contains songs written in various metres, is the source, for us, of the famous *Harmodius-Song*, and of the inimitable *War-Song* of Hybrias the Cretan, which has been translated once for all by Thomas Campbell. The *Drinking-Songs* ascribed to the Seven Sages and preserved by Diogenes Laertius may be as old as 500 B.C. Timocreon's *Song to Wealth* is to be dated about 470.

Side by side with these poems of love, wine, and wisdom, sung or recited, most of them, at table, the Greek genius developed the 'Inscription', or to use its own word, Epigram. This class, written almost entirely in Elegiac metre, came to include not only Epitaphs, Labels—called Dedications—for works of art and other votive offerings, and inscriptions for wells, gardens, banks, or inns, but title-poems for books, 'posies' or labels for gifts, invitations and other letters to friends, drinking-songs, love-songs, and short satirical poems. We have two or three Epigrams, in this sense, rather doubtfully ascribed to Sappho, we have some of Anacreon, many—some very lovely ones—of Simonides, two of Bacchylides, one of Aeschylus. The Alexandrian and later Ages have left us hundreds. The songs of Choral Lyric, danced and sung by a number of performers together, are mostly outside our present scope; but the reader will find here a fine fragment of Lycophronides; and one or two exquisite fragments of Sappho's *Epithalamies* and Alcman's *Maiden-Songs*, and a few examples from Simonides, including his incomparable *Danaë*—these to be recognised as choral by the uneven length of the lines—are reserved for a later volume.

[5]

Of Greek Folk-Song—there is really no difference between folk-song and other poetry, save perhaps in its uses and the manner of its transmission, but the distinction is generally made—it is hoped to include one of the pretty Children's Game-Songs, and the delightful *Swallow-Song*, which after two thousand years still survives in a modernised form in Thessaly. Of the fragments of the philosophers I have translated for a later volume Xenophanes' lines on Anthropomorphism and Scythînus' on Time—both amazingly modern—and a cynical couplet of the dramatist-philosopher Epicharmus.

In the latter half of the fifth century before Christ the tradition of poetry-of-the-table was carried on by Ion of Chios, Dionysius Chalcus, Evênus, and Critias; love inspired the *Lydè* of Antimachus: but we possess nothing of theirs that is 'universal' enough in its appeal to be given here. A few fine epitaphs, however, of this age have been translated, and a little poem of the painter Parrhasius, which serves to remind us that poetry had now come to be written by others than poets. Among the poems of the next century, we possess of Plato, always a poet, at least one supremely beautiful epitaph, and several superb little Love-Poems, of which some, strangely enough, seem to have been written for Socrates. Two epitaphs on Plato—he died in 347—one of them by Speusippus his successor at the Academy, belong to this period. Some of the Anonymous poems, too, other than those preserved in 'Theognis' and the collections cited by Athenaeus and Diogenes Laertius, are as old as the Athenian Age or older.

Hitherto, with the exception of Theognis, of whom we possess medieval MSS., we have been mainly dependent for our matter on the citations made by prose-authors. Henceforward, save for the Bucolic Poets and the inscriptions taken from existing stones, our sole sources, with a very few exceptions, are the two great collections, partly identical, made, the one by Constantine Cephalas in the tenth century, called the *Palatine Anthology*, and the other by Maximus Planûdes in 1301—written and dated in the author's own hand—called the *Planudean*. These include the earlier collections made by Meleâger, Philippus, Diogenian of Heracleia, Strato, and Agathias, between about 100 B.C. and about A.D. 560.

To the first part of the backward-looking newly-romantic Alexandrian Age, or to the almost equally studious but more prosaic generation which preceded it, belong the four woman poets, Erinna, Nossis, Moero, and Anytè; Antagoras, and probably Thymocles; Simmias or Simias, author of that delightful epitaph on Sophocles; Philêtas, teacher of Theocritus, inspirer—long afterwards—of Propertius, and the writer of at least one perfect epitaph; Nîcias, Theocritus' doctor-friend, husband of the lady of *The Distaff*; Asclepiades and Phalaecus, who gave their names to the Asclepiad and Hendecasyllabic metres; Hêdylus; probably Diotîmus, to whom we owe the beautiful lines on the poor cowherd; Posîdippus, better remembered for his 'fancy-epitaph' on Doricha—written perhaps for a statue—than for his pessimistic verses on life; the sympathetic but sometimes too learned Leonidas of Tarentum; the great Callimachus; and the greater Theocritus. The two last do not confine themselves in their shorter poems to the epigrammatic form; both imitate the matter and manner of Sappho

❡ *Epigrams from the* Planudean Anthology *are numbered according to their place in what is called the* Planudean Appendix, *a modern compilation including only the poems which are not now found in the* Palatine Anthology. *The* Planudean *was first printed in* 1494 *and the* Palatine *in* 1607.

[7]

and Alcaeus, and among those of Theocritus, at any rate, we have Love-Poems which, if archaistic in form, come none the less from the heart as well as the head. One of these is in hexameters, and this is the metre used by his imitators in the Pastoral, the sweet but sometimes too precious Sicilian Moschus, who flourished in the second century, and the wholly delightful Bion of Smyrna, who is to be placed about a hundred years before Christ.

But we have gone too fast. After Theocritus come Theodôridas, writer of the best of all the epitaphs on sailors; Dionysius ('You with the roses'); Dioscorides, Theaetêtus, and Alcaeus of Messênè; in the next century, Pamphilus, Capito (if he is to be identified with the epic poet of that name), and the gentle and humorous Antipater of Sidon; Glaucus of Nîcopolis, Ariston (the lines to the mice), Tymnes (the pet bird's epitaph), perhaps Menecrates; and, contemporary with Bion, Diodôrus of Sardis, called Zônas.

Of the remaining poets whose work is given here or reserved for a later volume, the first in time as in taste and feeling is Meleâger of Gadara in Palestine. His work often has the new quasi-oriental flavour of Bion's *Lament for Adonis*; yet if he is unrestrained it is only as a Greek. He lived near the beginning of the last century before Christ. His fellow-countryman the philosopher and amorist Philo-dêmus, the friend of Cicero, the same whose philosophical books have been partly preserved for us by the lava of Vesuvius, lived later in the same century. Among the lesser lights of that age are Statyllius Flaccus, perhaps the friend of the younger Cato; Thyillus ('Aristion the dancing-girl'); Isidôrus of Aegae; Tullius Laurea, of whom we have a graceful epitaph on Sappho; Adaeus of Macedon (*The Old Ox*); Apollonidas (*Old Euphron's Prayer*); and probably Gauradas (*The Lover and Echo*). To the times of Augustus

[8]

and Tiberius belong Satyrus and Evênus (not to be con-
fused with his earlier namesake); Lollius Bassus, Alpheius
of Mytilene, and Antipater of Thessalonîca; Antiphanes;
Crinagoras, friend of the young Marcellus; the writer of at
least one vivid sea-piece, Antiphilus; Biânor, Automedon,
and the genial Marcus Argentarius. Later in the first
century of our era come Maecius and the satiric Nîcarchus;
Leonidas of Alexandria, who succeeds sometimes in spite
of his misguided ingenuity; Lucillius, pensioner of Nero;
Diotîmus of Milêtus; and probably Gaetulicus.

Of the age of Plutarch, Lucian, and Marcus Aurelius—
Gibbon's 'happy period', 96–180—I have translated some
pretty Love-Poems of Strato of Sardis, the compiler of the
collection known as *Musa Puerilis*, Book xii in the *Palatine
Anthology*; epigrams by two poets called Archias; a fine
little poem by Ptolemy the Astronomer; and some notable
verses of Lucian himself, including one perfect epitaph of
a child. Here too should be placed, in all probability, the
gay love-poet Rufînus.

Two generations after Constantine and the state-
recognition of Christianity in 324 come the still-Pagan
lover-moralist Palladas, friend of the woman-philosopher
who gives her name to Charles Kingsley's novel *Hypatia*;
and probably Aesôpus, the otherwise unknown author of
a fine address to Life. The remains of both these poets
suggest to us that they belonged to a tired world. Then there
is another gap in our story till the sixth century and the
revival of elegant verse under Justinian. The epigrams of
the court-officials Paulus and Irênaeus; of Macedonius the
Consul, Theodôrus the Proconsul, Julian Prefect of Egypt;
of the advocates Arabius (author of *The Palace-Garden*),
Leontius (*The Lucky Cup*), and probably Nîlus (*The
Laughing Satyr*); of one Eratosthenes, and Mariânus the

E   [9]   B

translator of Theocritus into iambics; were collected and edited with his own by the lawyer-historian Agathias. Some of these which remind us of our Elizabethans, particularly some of the sonnet-like love-poems of Macedonius, Paulus, and Agathias, deserve a higher epithet than 'elegant'. Indeed, with the exception of a few epitaphs, they show more real feeling than any short poem since Meleâger's. Whether the love-poems of these Byzantines have any connexion with the Italian origins of the Sonnet is a question which deserves to be investigated. The great movement of Greek books westward began in 1185.

'Epigrams' in the old language—as it now was—continued to be written in the ancient tradition for four centuries after Justinian. Comêtas the Chartulary, the latest writer whose work I have translated, was contemporary with the last 'ancient' editor but one of the *Anthology*, Constantine Cephalas, who was Protopapas or chief-priest at the court of Constantine VII only a century and a half before our Norman Conquest. From 650 B.C., when our story begins, to A.D. 920, when it ends, is nearly sixteen hundred years.

The Sources of the Poems

A.P. = *Anthologia Palatina*, *Plan.* its Planudean Appendix, *L.G.* = *Lyra Graeca* in the Loeb Classical Library, *E.I.* = *Elegy and Iambus* in the same, Dl. = Diehl *Anthologia Lyrica* in the Teubner series; for the Palatine Anthology and Appendix see Paton *Greek Anthology* in the Loeb Classical Library, and, for Books i–ix of the same, Stadtmüller *Anthologia Graeca Epigrammatum* in the Teubner series (subtracting one from all references to Book v); for the later Books, and Epigrams preserved elsewhere, see also Dübner *Anthologia Palatina etc.* in the Didot series.

THE SOURCES OF THE POEMS

Sappho

1

[*A Fragment*]

As the hyacinth which the shepherd tramples on the hill
Lies upon the ground and lying bloometh purple still...

2

[*A Fragment*]

I have a little daughter rare
That 's like the golden flowers fair,
    My Cleïs;
I would not take all Lydia wide,
No, nor lovely Greece beside
    For Cleïs.

3

[*A Fragment*]

I loved you, Atthis, long ago,
   While yet my youth was blossoming
And you were still, to outward show,
   A slight ungainly little thing.

3 *The second line is restored from a Latin paraphrase.*

Theognis

1

Love too in season riseth in the sky;
   When with Spring's bloom the earth is teeming, then
From Cyprus' beauteous isle he draweth nigh
   Bringing delight to all the sons of men.

2

Prowess and beauty fall to few 'neath heaven,
And happy he to whom they both be given;
Ev'ry man honours him; the young, the old,
They he grew up with, yield him place of right;
Respect grows with the years, and none so bold
To flout God's law nor man's in his despite.

3

Shun when you be gray and old
   A wife whose locks are raven:
Like boat whose anchors never hold
That ne'er obeys the helm aright,
She'll slip her moorings any night
   And make another haven.

4

Be patient, heart; you can't have all your due;
Others love beauty just as much as you.

1 *Cyprus was one of the chief seats of the worship of Aphrodite, who for this reason was often called Cypris, 'the Cyprian'.*   3 *Probably by a later hand.*

[16]

Anacreon

[*A Fragment*]

I should love to play with you;
You have a pretty way with you.

❦

Athenian Drinking-Song

I know what I should like to be,
    A pretty ivory lyre,
That a pretty lad might take me
    To play in Bacchus' quire.

❦

Bacchylides

[*A Fragment*]

Virtue to an upgrowing life lends grace
As master-painter to a lovely face.

❦

Plato

I

A DEDICATION TO APHRODITE

Laïs that laugh'd all Greece to scorn
And swarms of lovers kept forlorn,
Lady of Paphos, Queen divine,
Lays her mirror in Thy shrine;
To what she is she blind would be,
And what she was she cannot see.

2

The Graces sought a shrine that would never fall, and found
the soul of Aristophanes.

3

ON PRAXITELES' STATUE OF APHRODITE AT CNIDUS

Seeing her Cnidian self Cypris cried 'Hey!
'Where did Praxiteles see me naked, pray?'

4

EPITAPH

on his beloved friend Aster or 'Star'

Even as you shone once the Star of Morn among the
living, so in death you shine now the Star of Eve among
the dead.

2 *This poem, and a few others which will bear it, are here translated
into prose. Aristophanes died about 385 B.C. when Plato would be about
forty-two; this may be an epitaph but is not recorded as such.*

Lycophronides

In lad, in lass,
In buxom dame,
True beauty has
A modest face;
'Tis proper shame
Makes proper grace.

✒

Simmias

AN EPITAPH

Push soft and sure thy clinging green,
Ivy, o'er Sophocles' dear tomb,
Fold it, fond Vine, in your embrace,
And you, gay Rose, about it bloom,
For the wisdom sweet and keen
He learnt to wield of Muse and Grace.

✒

LYCOPHRONIDES: *The Greek* 'gold-bearing *lass' refers to the custom
by which free-born girls wore an ornament of gold, cf.* Aristophanes
Birds 670.   SIMMIAS: *Not a true epitaph; Sophocles died in* 406,
some generations before.

Anonymous

1

O were I a red rose,
   That your dear hands might tie me
Where breasts white as the snows
   Could not deny me!

Anonymous

2

I would I were a breeze, and you,
   Walking the shore apart,
Would bare your bosom when I blew
   And take me to your heart!

¶ *Anonymous poems are often undatable; in this selection, which is arranged chronologically, they are put where they seem to belong, but the guess may not always be right.*

Asclepiades

I

Snow if Thou wilt, hail if Thou'rt fain,
Lower, lighten, thunder, rain,
Shake earthward all Thy darkling wrack;
If, Lord, Thou slay me, I'll turn back:
But leave me life, and worse than this
Shall not stay me from my bliss;
My master 's Thine, who made Thee pass
To a bride-bed fenced with brass.

2

Be witness, Night—to-night you are not blind—,
    How treach'rous Nîco's Pythias can be:
I came invited; may you sometime find
    Her at my door saying the same of me.

3

Hermionè once play'd with me
    Girt with a flower'd zone o'erwrit
(Paphian Queen, I swear by Thee)
    With golden lettering, to wit—
'Love me and be not sore at heart
'If one of many loves thou art.'

1 *The* bride *is Danaĕ, to whom, when shut up by her father in a brazen
tower, Zeus came in the form of a shower of gold.*   2 Pythias *is
Nîco's daughter.*   3 *The* Paphian Queen *is Aphrodite; Paphos was
one of the chief seats of her worship.*

Asclepiades

4

A MAIDEN'S COMPLAINT OF ARCHEADES

My love was lovesick for me once; to-day
Even in sport he will not look my way:
Sweet Love Himself 's not always sweet, we know,
But, sour sometimes, doth all the sweeter grow.

5

Not two-and-twenty, yet
    Of life I tire;
Ye Loves, why do ye set
    Me all afire?
What would ye babies do
    If I should die?
Why ye'd play on, trust you,
    At toss-penny.

Anytè

A DEDICATION
for a statue and holy-place of Aphrodite the Sea-Born Goddess

This shall Cypris' precinct be;
Here for ever 'tis Her will
To stand and gaze from shore to sea
The sailor's homeward course to bless;
And the deep is awed and still
Looking on such loveliness.

4 Love, *when male in the Greek, is the Cupid of the Latin poets and their modern imitators; when female, his mother Aphrodite or Cypris.*

Theocritus

THE DISTAFF

The poet, sailing to Milêtus from his home at Syracuse, takes a gift for the newly married wife of his old friend the physician and poet Nîcias.

Distaff, to all good huswives gift of the Huswife above,
Friend of the loom and the spindle, come where the Lady of Love
Reigns 'mid the tall soft rushes in Nêleus' town so gay;
For thither I'm bound, Zeus willing; come let's aboard and away.
I shall see that dear good child of sweetness and music agen,
I shall see, and shall love as of old, Nîcias fondest of men;
And you, little ivory creature, whom cunning has bidden to be,
Shall make my gift to his goodwife. And ofttimes you and she
Shall spin fine yarn for the mantle my lord shall wear at the town,
And finer yarn for the stuff to make my lady's gown.
For the fleecy mothers of flocks may bring their coats to the shears
Twice between June and June, for aught pretty Theugenis cares,
Such a marvel she is of discretion, so busy a body is she;
And no slovenly do-nought dame should ever have had you of me;
For we're countrymen—both of the town old Archias built in the
    west,
The apple of Sicily's eye, home of her bravest and best.
But now you'll lodge at a wiseacre's mighty with manifold spells
Us of the flesh to defend from the ills of the flesh—who dwells
At Milêtus, Ionian, lovely; and so, when her neighbours see,
They'll wish they'd Theugenis' distaff, and then you'll remind her
    maybe
Of her poet-guest. 'Great love'—thus often the tale will be told—
'Goes with a little gift, and all from a friend is gold.'

¶ The Huswife above *is Athena.*   *Syracuse was founded by Archias of Corinth.*

Thymocles

I prophesied to thee (dost mind the time?)
'Nothing's so fair or fleet as beauty's prime;
'The swiftest bird is tardier': and now see
Where all the petals of thy flower be.

Posîdippus

1

If she's engaged I'll go away,
    If not, I want one minute;
Do let me in; for password say
    The street had footpads in it,
But lusty Love has seen me through 'em
Although my victuals wine had to 'em.

2

Doricha, beloved by Sappho's brother, was a courtesan of the Greeks'
Egyptian port Naucratis, which was separated from the sea by a series
of lagoons through which flowed the Canopic outfall of the Nile.

Doricha, 'tis but bone they now adorn,
The dainty snood that bound your braids of old,
And that balm-breathing robe that used to fold
The fair Charaxus to you till 'twas morn;
But the white speaking scroll of Sappho's song
Lives and will live. Happy your memory,
Which Naucratis will treasure here so long
As ships steer up Nile's fairway from the sea.

1 *For* she *the Greek has Pythias.*   2 Doricha *is mentioned by*
Sappho in a poem of which we possess four short lines; this, like many of
the more elaborate epitaphs given below, is a mere tour de force.

Posîdippus

3

TO LOVE

Love, I'm well arm'd; I'll fight thee to a fall,
   Though I'm no God; call off the attack:
If drunk shouldst find me, take me for thy thrall;
   Sober, I've Reason at my back.

4

TO PHILAENIS

Think not to cozen me, my dear,
   Though suasive tears your eyes bedim;
With me, you love me best, 'tis clear,
   And with another, him.

Capito

When pretty looks lack pretty ways,
All men stare and no man stays;
Ways must needs enable looks,
For baits float idle without hooks.

Moschus

When Alphêus fresh from Pisa
                                runs out beyond the land
To lead his Arethuse the stream
                                that 's fed wild olives there,
And with it, for a bridegift,
                                leaves, flow'rs, and sacred sand,
Then down he sinks into the deep
                                all underseas to fare;
And salt and sweet the waters
                                are divided each from each,
And Ocean 's none the wiser
                                for either gift or giver;
And so that impish trap-setter
                                who fearsome love can teach,
Has taught the art of diving
                                to a love-enchanted river.

¶ Arethusa: *the famous fountain of Syracuse.* *The* wild olive *made the wreath of victory in the Olympic Games, which were held at Pisa in the Peloponnese, and the* sacred sand *is the sand of the holy ground they were held in, while the* leaves *and* flowers *suggest the flower-pelting with which the spectators honoured the victors.* Greek rivers, *when in flood, are recognisable far out at sea.*

Antipater of Sidon

I

A YOUNG WIFE'S DEDICATION TO APHRODITE

E'en as she vow'd, Bithynian Cytherè
Gives You Yourself in stone, great Love-Lady:
Grant much for little, as You're wont to do;
Her husband's love is all she asks of You.

2

AN EPITAPH

Thou hast thy Sappho, fond Aeolian earth,
The mortal Muse that adds one to the Nine,
Whom Love and Love's dear Son, her friends from birth
Taught with Persuasion's aid a wreath to twine
Of fame unfading for her Greece and thee:
O when, ye Fates, a life your spindle twirl'd
That gave eternal music to the world,
Why twired ye not therein eternity?

1 *A marble statuette would not be so costly as one of bronze or silver.*   2 *Perhaps written for a statue.*

[27]   D 2

Meleâger

1

OF ANDRAGATHUS

The winds that blow so kindly
               to ships that Northward roll,
Have taken, O ye lovers,
               the love that 's half my soul.

Thrice happy are the ships, methinks,
               thrice happy is the sea,
And more than thrice the winds happy,
               to take my love from me.

O would I were a dolphin
               that my love might ride me o'er,
And land among the lovely lads
               upon the Rhodian shore!

2

TO HIS LADY

I 've found you out; don't swear like that;
    I know about that visit;
I know, I say, what you 've been at:
    That's how it is, then, is it?

You sleep alone do you still say,
    You story-telling baby?
Just hear her, at this time of day!
    Not with great Cleon? or maybe —?

1 *Lovers of Horace should compare the third Ode of his First Book;
he seems to have known Meleâger's poems.*

Meleâger

But what 's the use of threat'ning? Go,
  You flea that spoils my sleep, you!
And yet you're off to *him*, I know;
  So, tit for tat, I'll keep you.

3

The flowers fade on Hêliodôra's brow;
Once they adorn'd her, she adorns them now.

4

TO APHRODITE

Meleâger dedicates
  His playmate lamp, dear Love, to Thee;
'Tis one of the initiates
  In Thy midnight mystery.

5

THE LOVE-MESSAGE

Take this message, Dorcas; eh?
  Take 't again; what? take 't again;
Haste, be quick; nay, Dorcas, stay;
  Are you sure you have it plain?

Pray add—nay (I'm a fool), say nought,
  Nay, only this; nay, say all, do;
Mind, ev'ry word—yet why be taught,
  When your teacher goes with you?

5 Dorcas is his mistress's maid.

[29]

Meleâger

6

OF HÊLIODÔRA

Long hence they'll tell in history how of yore
The Graces were outgraced by Heliodore.

7

TO TIMARION

A kiss of birdlime, eyes of fire thou hast;
Look at me, and I burn; touch me, and I'm held fast.

8

Portly ocean-riding galleons
      down the Hellespont that go,
Taking to your swelling bosoms
      any southward airs that blow,
Should you spy my Phanion gazing
      seaward from the Coän strand,
Tell her that her true-love's coming
      by the long way of the land:
So, if these be welcome tidings,
      you shall win such tidings' meed;
Zeus shall breathe into your canvas
      all the favouring winds you need.

7 Timarion: *Greek women's names often have the neuter suffix* -ion; *originally perhaps such names were endearing diminutives like ours with suffix* -y *or* -ie.　8 *He is going round through Asia Minor to cross to Cos by the ferry; the ships are bound, perhaps, for Egypt.*

Meleâger

9

Twy-wing'd unconscionable brood,
Shrill night-riders that suck our blood,
Pray let my darling sleep a wink
While of myself I give you drink.

But vain my plea; for such soft skin
E'en brutes like you love snuggling in:
Yet take my warning, imps, or you
Shall know what jealous hands can do.

10

OF HIS FRIEND PRAXITELES

The old Praxiteles live form did give
To stone, and in dumb show soft beauty grave;
His living namesake, conj'ring things that live,
Hath grav'n within me Love, the Almighty Knave:
Albeit in name the new 's the old, in merit
Perchance he 's more, shaping not stone but spirit;
Now may it please him so to mould my mind
That this his Love may fitly there be shrined.

Meleâger

11

I keep a ball-player; it 's Love, dear Sue;
And look, he throws my beating heart at you:
Come, play with him; if you don't throw it back,
You'll wish you had the sportsmanship you lack.

12

Cricket that tipsy with a drop of dew
   To the wide landscape blab your tuneful din,
On the tree-tops, though none should hear but you,
   Fiddling with saw-like legs on swarthy skin,

Play to regale the Maidens of the Glade
   New notes that time with Pan's own pipe will keep,
That I, reclined beneath the plane-tree's shade,
   May 'scape from Love and sleep the noontide sleep.

13

O Night, O Stars, O lover-lighting Moon,
And Lute my fellow-serenader, say,
Shall I my mistress find awake, alone,
And weeping to her lamp her eyes away?
Or lies she double, and must these flow'rs of mine
Hang, tear-wet suppliants, as before Love's shrine,
Inscribed 'These love-spoils, Cypris, at Thy gate
'Gave Meleâger, Thy initiate'?

11 *In line* 3 *the Greek is* '*if you throw me away*', *i.e. not back to the thrower as willing to play. In the Greek,* Sue *is Heliodora.*   13 *It was the custom for lovers to hang up the wreath worn at the dinner-table beside their beloved's door if refused admission.*

Meleâger

14

Love 's moulded in me sweet-voiced Heliodore
To be soul of my soul for evermore.

15

If I see Thêron, all the world I see;
If all but Thêron, 'tis a blank to me.

16

Saucy Asclêpias with her calm blue eyes
Woos every man to sail on love's emprise.

17

My ears with Love keep ever singing, singing,
And my dumb eyes to Pain sweet water bringing;
No respite have I now by light nor dark;
Sure, the spell works; my heart must bear its mark:
Wing'd Loves, have you the wit to fly to men,
Yet lack all pow'r to fly away agen?

---

17 Loves: *in Alexandrian literature, as in Pompeian paintings, Cupid is often plural.*

18

TO LOVE

By Cypris, Love, they all shall go,
Arrows, arrow-case, and bow;
I'll burn 'em, s'help me. Why d'ye sniggle,
Turn your nose up, grin, and giggle?
The laugh 's on t'other side, I'll lay:
Those quills that show Desire the way
I'll clip, those feet with steel entwine.—
Yet Pyrrhic triumph will be mine
If wolf so near the fold I tie;
So don your shoes, spread wing, and fly:
Seek other foes, resistless elf,
I've had enough of you myself.

19

OF ZÊNOPHILA

Oyez, oyez! 'tis hue and cry
    For naughty Love; before 'twas morn
He left his bed and off did fly:
    His tears are joy, his smiles are scorn;
He 's pert, he 's quick, his tongue wags free;
    He bears a bow and goes with wings.
Whose 'tis, I know not; Heav'n, Earth, Sea,
    Disown this foe of men and things:
Look to yourselves; for I'll be bound,
    In wait for some poor soul he lies:
Aha! I spy him; imp, you're found;
    You're ambush'd in my loved one's eyes.

19 *The lover speaks as town-crier.*

[34]

Meleâger

20

OF MYISCUS

By Love, they're fair, the sons of Tyre; but one
Puts all the stars out like the uprisen Sun.

21

TO MYISCUS

The weather 's rough, but Love and his sweet pain
  Bear me on Revel's racing tide to thee:
The storm 's Desire, the sea 's the Cyprian main;
  Let me cast anchor where I fain would be.

Philodêmus

I

TO LYSIDICÈ

Thy summer 's in the bud, my dear,
  Thy virgin grapes yet green,
But the Loves their shafts are whetting
  And a fire burns unseen.

Before they string their bows, my dear,
  We lovers all must fly,
Or there'll be a conflagration
  Whose smoke will reach the sky.

2

Fill up the lamp with liquor, Joan,
  (See it may, but will not tell)
And go; live witness Love would none.
  Mind, wench, the latch. And now, sweet Nell—;
You, kind bed, the lover's friend,
Shall hear Love's story to the end.

3

Her speaking eyes, her flowing wit,
  Her skill to sing or play—
Xanthippè's flame so newly lit,
  Will burn thee, heart, some day:
Ask me not where, nor when, nor how;
The smoke will tell thee soon enow.

2 Joan, *the maid as in Shakespeare, in the Greek is Philaenis, and* Nell, *the mistress, Xantho.*

Philodêmus

4

Though she 's so short and dark, her hair
Like Nemean diadem is curl'd;
Her skin, no down is tenderer,
Her voice, 't would love-bewitch the world;
And though she gives me all she 's got,
To ask she oft remembers not:
Love keep me this Philainion
Till I can find a better one.

5

Betty and Belle will surely be
    The death of me:
Pretty Belle knows Love too well,
Pretty Bet knows him not yet;
One touch I may, the other nay:
Which of the two 's the best to woo
By Love I swear I know not.—There,
Both are pretty, but I'll take Betty:
Good meat is always on the board,
    The best is stor'd.

Anonymous

3

Blow not upon thy torch, whoe'er thou art,
To light thy lamp at; light it at my heart.

4 *For* Nemean diadem *the Greek has* 'parsley', *for* love-bewitch the
world '*more magical than the cestus*' (*the Girdle of Aphroditε, embroidered
with love-spells*).   5 *The Greek says Thermion and Demonoē.*

Statyllius Flaccus

I am the silver lamp a simple fellow
   Gave, faithful witness of her nights to be,
To the unfaithful Napè, by whose pillow
   I flicker now ashamed of what I see:
Sleepless you lie, man, sick and sore at heart;
We both are burning, but, woe 's me! apart.

Gauradas

THE LOVER AND ECHO

Wilt grant a favour if I name it?
               —Name it.
I love, but doubt if she's not shy.
               —Not shy.
Then I've the right if I could claim it.
               —Claim it.
Then tell her for her love sigh I.
               —Ay, ay.
I have a little gift to make her.
               —Make her.
Then all that's left to do 's to take her.
               —Take her.

GAURADAS: *Line 4 has a pun on* ἐρῶ '*I love*' *and* ἐρῶ '*I will say or* tell'; *the translation has a similar play upon words in the next line.*

Antipater of Thessalonîca

I

Here 's Eurôpa for a shilling;
No one minds, and she's quite willing;
Spotless sheets her charms enfold,
She'll light a fire if it be cold:
No need to have turn'd bull, dear Jove,
The day you sought Eurôpa's love.

2

FOR A STATUE

Sappho 's my name; all women I outvie
As Homer doth all men in poesy.

3

The dawn is red, Chrysilla; long ago
    The eager cock first cried the jealous day;
Curst bird! thou'rt jealous too, to treat me so,
    Driving me out to hear fools say their say:
Art growing old, Tithônus? thou hast sped
Thy mate, methinks, full early from thy bed.

Evênus

PRAXITELES' STATUE OF APHRODITE AT CNIDUS

When her two Rivals saw the Cnidian's beauty,
'We're wrong' cried they; 'poor Paris did his duty.'

3 Tithônus, *to whom the Gods gave immortality without perpetual youth,
was husband of Dawn.*   Evênus: *The Judgment of Paris.*

[39]

Marcus Argentarius

I

Though 't be spices ten times over,
    Sweet-breath'd Isias, still to sleep,
Wake, and take the gift a lover
    Asks your own dear hand to keep.

Take this wreath for your adorning
    While 'tis in its flow'ring-time:
'Twill be past it by the morning,
    Like you maidens past your prime.

2

OF DIOCLEIA

A slender Cypris in my fair you'll see,
    For all she be with inward beauty blest;
And yet the less between us, her and me,
    The nigher will her heart be to my breast.

3

OF ANTIGONÈ

Dear Lamp, thy sputtering 's a sneeze,
    And sneezes can foretell:
Thou'st sputter'd thrice; there 's luck in threes;
    Comes she I love so well?
If so, Lord, stand in Phoebus' shrine
And to His oracles add thine.

3 *He will dedicate him to Apollo.*

[40]

Marcus Argentarius

4

OF PYRRHA

Poring once o'er Hesiod
  I heard my love the doorlatch raise;
I cast him down and cried ''Fore God!
  'Why read thy Works and waste my Days?'

Diotîmus of Milêtus

TO A DUENNA

Nursie dear,
  When I come near,
Why d'you bark at me like this?
  Why d'you double
  All my trouble
When you lead a pretty miss?

All I do
  'S to follow you,
As my proper ways I go,
  Looking at her;
  Does it matter?
Men may look at Gods, you know.

Lucillius

In conjugating *love*, take, Love, your choice;
Miss it all out or add the passive voice.

4 *Hesiod's most famous poem is the* Works and Days.

Gaetulicus

A DEDICATION

to Aphrodite the Sea-Born Goddess

Here I bring what gift I may,
    Guardian of the Beach, to Thee,
These simnels; for at break of day
    I cross the broad Ionian Sea
To seek my Idothea's breast:
    O Cypris, let Thy favour shine
Both on my course and on my quest,
    For beach and bride-bed both are thine.

Strato

1

Try as I will to pass
    A pretty lass,
Before I'm gone a yard
    I'm staring hard.

2

OF MOERIS

At even when good-nights are said,
He kiss'd me; was it in a dream?
All else stays clearly in my head,
What questions put, what answers given;
But still that kiss doth doubtful seem—
Can this be earth that then was heaven?

[42]

Strato

3

If I wouldn't, you kiss me;
 If I would, then you fly:
You are kind if you miss me,
 And coy if I'm by.

4

Beauty that brags should mind the rose,
That fades and to the dunghill goes;
A flow'ret's bloom, a beauty's prime,
Are wither'd both by envious Time.

5

You've cast your hook, and I am on;
 If you would play me, play:
But stand your ground, child; if you run
 'Tis odds I get away.

Anonymous

4

TO APHRODITE

I loved, great Love, I snatch'd a kiss,
I ask'd, she gave, and it was bliss;
But who she is, whose child, or how
'Twas as it was, none knows but Thou.

Anonymous

5

AN EPITAPH

Ripe and ready for love's best
   Thou'st shut those gentle eyes of thine:
Gone 's the song, the 'witching jest,
   The saucy pledging of the wine:
Stern Death, why take our lovely Nell?
Wast thou in love with her as well?

Archias

Flee Love? 'tis labour lost; can I
Escape afoot what 's wing'd to fly?

5 For Nell *the Greek has Patrophila.*

Rufinus

1

Delia's beauty—well it may—
Turns her head; to my 'Good day'
  No reply she'll render,

But lifts her eyebrows, and no more:
The flow'rs I hang above her door
  Seem only to offend her;

She stamps on them in ire sublime:
Hasten, wrinkles; hasten, Time;
  You, at least, can bend her.

2

OF MAEONIS

When Pallas and Hera beheld my sweet rose,
They cried—and they meant it—' Let's keep on our clothes;
'To lose the prize once was a slap in the face,
'To lose it again would be lasting disgrace.'

3

TO LOVE THE TORCHBEARER

If two together 's past your wit,
  Linkman, howe'er you try it,
Put out, my boy, the link you've lit
  Or light the other by it.

1 *For* Delia *the Greek has Rhodopè.*   2 *The Judgment of Paris.*

[45]

Rufinus

4

Cypris bathing, as I live!
    And all her lovelocks flowing;
Mercy, Queen of Love; forgive
    Eyes that saw unknowing:

Now I see, it is not she,
    But Rhodoclea; dearest!
Whence this beauty? can they be
    Cypris' charms thou wearest?

5

I send you, pretty Rosalind,
A garland fair my hands have twined;
Here 's rosebuds for you if you will,
Wet windflow'r, dewy daffodil,
Lily and dark-ey'd violet—
O take them for your coronet,
And put that haughty look away:
You flow'r and fade as well as they.

Lucian

A VOTIVE STATUE OF APHRODITE

This lovely likeness, Cypris, take; 'tis Thine:
I could not bring aught better to Thy shrine.

5 For Rosalind *the Greek has Rhodoclea.*

Macedonius the Consul

1

The vintage cometh once a year, and none,
Plucking the grape, the tendril's twine disdains:
When I, with thee, my thought's delight, made one,
Hold rose-blush beauty fast in yielding chains
And pluck my grapes, I cannot bide till Spring,
Let alone Autumn, for fresh harvesting,
So full of fruit art thou: e'en so, my dear,
Mayst thou be ripe to vintage all life's year;
And if wry wrinkles o'er thee twining go,
Then twine they may, because I love thee so.

2

You whinny like a lovesick foal,
    You nod and beck, but all in vain;
I've sworn, hard heart, upon my soul,
    I'll never smile at you again.

Keep to yourself, make lonely play,
    Pout idle lips to meet the air;
For I shall go another way;
    There's better love-makers elsewhere.

3

Once in the reeling riot-throng
   She clash'd the Bacchant gold,
And skipp'd it fair the fair among;
   But now she 's sick and old.

They shrink and pass, who for love's boon
   Once supplicating stood;
Conjunction miss'd, the waxing moon
   Has been eclips'd for good.

4

TO A LYRE-GIRL

Thy cheeks are roses and thy lips delight,
   Thy fingers Music make and Love thine eyes,
Thy song leads hearing captive, thy look sight,
   And all thou art takes youth for prey and prize.

Agathias

1

She that in beauty held her head so high,
She that for pride her braided tresses tost
Fain with her vaunts my anguish to defy,
Is old and wrinkled now, and her charm lost,
Slack breasts, lank eyebrows, eyesight all but gone,
Her speech the dim lip-labour of a crone:
Gray hair for Love's own Nemesis I hold;
'Tis a just judge; the proud grow earliest old.

2

Enough 's a plenty, wisdom thinks:
   I, self-named a proper lad,
Wooing, as methought, a minx,
   Won her, or meseem'd I had.

Alack! she play'd the high and haughty,
   Sorry that she'd been too kind,
And I, the hectoring will-be-naughty,
   Know that pride is only wind.

Ev'rything 's turn'd arsy-versy;
   On repentant knees I cry,
'Sweetest saint, I pray you mercy;
   'Twas my youth that sinn'd, not I.'

¶ *Agathias seems to have been a younger contemporary of Paul the*
Silentiary, but his poems are put here so that his seventh may precede
Paul's first.

Agathias

3

FOR A LOVE-GIFT

I bring this kerchief, Best and Loveliest,
Bright with the needle's golden draughtsmanship;
Pray fling it o'er thy lovelocks, that it slip
Adown thy shoulders till it frame thy breast,
Thy lily breast, and clasp it close, and be
Its nuzzling babe; for thou art yet a maid,
And 'tis a maiden's: soon mayst thou be laid
In bridal sheets, and love's full harvest see;
Then will I bring to crown thy woman's life,
Gem-wov'n, the coif that speaks the wedded wife.

4

OF AN ACTRESS-MUSICIAN

When Ariadnè strokes the strings
Terpsichorè wins but by a head;
When stage with her full chest-note rings,
Melpomenè seems there instead;
And in a modern beauty-test

---

3 *The* kerchief *or head-shawl seems to have two long narrow or twisted ends which are to be crossed between and beneath the breasts and tied behind the back. I take line 6 as describing some way in which mothers carried their babies in a fold of their dress; some, however, take* ἐπιμάζιον *not as 'babe at breast' but as 'upon or round the breasts'.*
4 Terpsichorè *was the Muse of song and dance; lyre-players danced as they played:* Melpomenè *was the Muse of Tragedy.   In Greece, with its open-air theatres, actors and singers were praised for the loudness of their voices.*

Agathias

Cypris would be second best
And Paris' finding quash'd.—But oh!
Not a word of this, you know,
Or Bacchus will come down to woo
Ariadnè Number Two.

5

What means this sigh?
      —Love, more 's the pity.
—Whose?
    —A maiden's.
      —Is she pretty?
—Yes, to me.
    —Where met?
      —At dinner
Side by side.
    —D'ye hope to win her?
—*Sub rosa.*
    —Why not make a match?
—Reckon'd by fortune she 's no catch.
—Reckon'd? then love 's no word for it;
Love 's of the heart not of the wit.

4 *The reference is to the Judgment of Paris.*

Agathias

6

A DEDICATION

This fallow plot Strato the husbandman
Gives for his kindness to the highland Pan:
Feed flock here, Pan; here let a landlord's eye
Rove where no more the share shall cleaving go;
A lucky farm 'tis, too; I'll tell thee why:—
Echo will be thy bride, she loves it so.

7

TO PAUL THE SILENTIARY

from the far side of the Bosporus, whither the writer had withdrawn to study law.

Here earth is green with springing wood
And all the leaf's rich grace display'd;
Here birds that mother many a brood
Call beneath the cypress shade;
The goldfinch trills, and from his brere
The tree-frog murmurs: yet for me
What joys are these? I'd rather hear
Thy voice than Phoebus' magic string.
Two longings have I, one for thee,
Blest friend, one for the tenderling
I burn to think of: but alas!
Far must I bide; Law holds the pass.

6 *The Greek has the longer form of the name, Stratonîcus.*   7 *The* tree-frog *is a little tree-climbing toad, called in the south of France 'demoiselle'; it was a great favourite.*

Paul the Silentiary

1

Replying to the above

Love knows no Law; when love 's to do
No other work can keep us busy:
If law's pursuit is what keeps you,
Then Love 's not in your heart, friend, is he?
What love is his yon narrow firth
Bars from the bed he knows so well?
Leander show'd his love's true worth
Those nights he swam it; if you're burning,
There 's the ferry: truth to tell,
You've giv'n up love, my lad, for learning:
Love 's Cypris' work, Athena's law;
Servant of both I never saw.

2

I seek to say farewell, yet rein
    My utt'rance back and stay beside thee;
Like the dark of Hell's domain
    I shun what from me must divide thee.

Thy light 's like day's: yet day's is dumb;
    Thine, all my heart's dear hopes a-bringing,
Doth with a spoken music come
    Sweeter than any Siren's singing.

---

1 *Leander, in the story, swam the Bosporus every night to visit his beloved, Hero.*

Paul the Silentiary

3

TO RHODOPÈ

Let 's kiss, Beloved, on the sly,
  Of Love's dear craft a myst'ry making;
'Tis sweet to outwit the watchful eye,
  And stolen nights are best for waking.

4

The rose no garland needs, nor thou, my queen,
A coif with gems befringed, a robe with vair;
No pearl outpeers the lustre of thy skin,
Nor gold the glory of thy unbraided hair;
Jacinths of Ind that like thwart sunbeams show,
'Fore thy twin flashings, dim to their eclipse;
Thy bosom's honey'd concent, thy dew'd lips,
Outlure Love's magic-purfled zone: blent so
These beauties whelm me, save that from thine eyes
There looks the comfort of a sweet surmise.

5

OF LAÏS

Her smile is sweet, my dearest dear's,
But sweet, my friends, the very tears
That from those twinkling eyes are shed:
Last night when long she'd leant her head
Upon my shoulder, came a sigh

4 Love's zone: *the Girdle of Aphrodite, embroidered with love-spells.*

[54]

Paul the Silentiary

For nought; I kiss'd; as our lips met,
A drop from some clear fountain wet
Our kissing for us; ask'd for why,
'For fear' said she 'you leave me lorn;
'You men are all deceivers born.'

6

Out upon it, pretty Nance,
　　How your duenna eyes me!
Your gentle speech, your whisp'ring glance
　　Her jealous watch denies me;

She beats the many-ey'd patrol
　　Of Argus in the fable;
Rage on, you spying beldam; soul
　　To eye 's impenetrable.

7

Be thy hair coif'd, with love I pine—
'Tis tower'd Cybelè's, not thine:
Uncoif'd, its 'mazing gold, my sweet,
Scares my ten wits from their seat;
Untie and 'neath white kerchief pin it,
There's all as fierce a heartburn in it:
Three Graces tend its fashions three;
However drest 'tis fire to me.

6 No name is given in the Greek.

[55]

Paul the Silentiary

8

Last night when merry and out for love
   Flow'rs for her door I brought her,
Hermonassa from above
   Emptied a cup of water.

My hair, that might so well trimm'd up
   Have lasted days, she drench'd it;
Yet water from her own sweet cup
   Fann'd my flame, not quench'd it.

9

E'en Tantalus below, methinks, bears less
   Of torment for his sin than I unsinning;
He never saw my lady's loveliness
   Only to find her rosebud kiss past winning;
He weeps for ever, true, and the o'erhung stone
   Is there to dread; yet twice he cannot die;
But I both live love-worn to skin and bone
   And from my ebbing strength know death is nigh.

10

OF HIMSELF

He that once frown'd so bold and high
The plaything of a girl doth lie;
Who thought to crush a worm, instead
Hangs a foil'd and minish'd head;

[56]

Paul the Silentiary

'Tis he now bends the womanish knee,
The manly wrath 's now thine, not his;
Though, lioness, just thine anger be,
'Ware pride; thou'st look'd on Nemesis.

I I

FOR THE PORTRAIT OF A LYRE-GIRL
The aspiring brush hath caught thy beauty's grace;
O could it but thy sweet clear tones express,
That as eyes felt the glory of thy face,
So ears might feel thy music's loveliness!

Anonymous

6

EPITAPH ON A LOVELY BOY
Found on a tomb of about A.D. 100 *and placed here out of chronological order.*

Death in itself 's not bitter; all must die;
'Tis death untimely that 's worth weeping for:
Ungrown, unwed, beneath this stone I lie,
The love of many, to be loved of more.

Notes on the Text

Emendations marked *E* the translator believes to be his own.

Sappho 2: One word is missing from the Greek; it is more probably 'Lesbos' than 'Greece'; cf. Mosch. 3. 89.

Theognis 1: Reading χάρμα and γῆς (*E*) for σπέρμα and γῆν; σπέρμα must be an emendation *in mal. part.*

Simmias: Preferring εὐεπίης to εὐμαθίης, and reading ἤσκησ' ἐν (*E*) 'practised at the school of' for ἤσκησεν.

Anonymous 2: Reading with Schneidewin ἀγὰς for αὐγὰς.

Asclepiades 2: Reading after Hecker ἀλαὸν for ἄλλην.

Posîdippus 1: Reading εἰσκαλέσαι with Dilthey for ἐκκαλέσαι.

   2: Reading ἁπαλῆς κόσμησ' ἀπόδεσμα (*E*) for ἁπαλὰ κοιμήσατο δεσμῶν, περιστείλασα (*E*) for περιστέλλουσα, Σαπφῴας, and ἔστ' ἀνίῃ Νείλου ναῦς ἔφαλος τενάγη.

   4: Reading πιθανοῖς with Reiske for πιθανῶς, and δακρύοισι with Bothe for δάκρυσι.

Meleager 5: Reading τά γ' ἅπαντα λέγειν with Salmasius and Reiske for τὰ πάντα λέγε.

   8: Reading καλαὶ νέες ὥς in line 5 with Meineke for καλὴ νοὲς ὥς.

  11: τρέφω 'I keep (as one of my slaves)'; reading in line 4 οἴσει for οἴσω as Stadtmüller suggests.

  12: Preferring ἀγρονόμον.

  13: Reading ἀποκλαομένην with Huschke for ἀποδαομένην in line 4, and δὲ ῥάνας with Hecker for μαράνας in line 5.

  17: Reading ἐκοίμισέ μ' (*E*) for ἐκοίμισεν or ἐκοίμανεν.

  21: Reading βαρὺ with Jacobs for βαρὺς.

Philodêmus 2: Keeping φίλη in line 5.

  5: Reading with Kaibel Δημονόη for Δημώ· ἡ.

Strato 5: Reading προέηκας with Jacobs for πεποίηκας.

Anonymous 4: τίς is clearly the girl, and so is ἧς, for the daughters of ἑταῖραι were called μητρόθεν.

Macedonius 1: Reading in line 6 βοτρύων (*E*) for χαρίτων, an obvious gloss.

[59]

Macedonius 3: Keeping χρυσεοκροτάλῳ and reading σπατάλη
with Brunck for σπατάλην, and τριλλίστῳ γ' with Bothe for
τριλλίστως.

4: Reading θάλλει with Jacobs for βάλλει.

Agathias 3: Taking τήνδε in line 4 as 'attracted' for τόδε (sc. τὸ
κρήδεμνον), and reading στήθεος ἆσσον (E) for στήθεϊ μᾶλλον
(στήθεϊ came from the line above, and ἆσσον is often cor-
rupted).

Paul the Silentiary 4: Reading στήθεος with Hecker for ἤθεος in
line 8.

5: Reading καὶ αὐτὸ for κατ' αὐτῶν as Waltz suggests.

Index of Poets

WITH DATES AND SOURCES

The date is the *floruit*, about the 40th year. References are given on pp. 11–13.

[61]

English Index of First Words

with references to the second edition of Mackail's *Select Epigrams from the Greek Anthology* and the *Oxford Book of Greek Verse.*

I

Greek Index of First Words

12

For EU product safety concerns, contact us at Calle de José Abascal, 56–1°, 28003 Madrid, Spain or eugpsr@cambridge.org.

www.ingramcontent.com/pod-product-compliance
Ingram Content Group UK Ltd.
Pitfield, Milton Keynes, MK11 3LW, UK
UKHW012327130625
459647UK00009B/114